HEBA

THE

HO'OPONOPONOIST

By Charan Surdhar

British Library Cataloguing Publication Data.
A catalogue record for this book is available from the British Library

ISBN 978-09564-8510-6

Published by Gurcharan K Surdhar in conjunction with

Authors OnLine Ltd
19 The Cinques
Gamligay, Sandy
Bedfordshire SG19 3NU
England

This book is also available in e-book format, details of which are available at www.authorsonline.co.uk

ii

This childrens fictional book contains material on childhood issues. The techniques followed in this book by the character "Heba" have been highlighted as a way a child can address these issues. The material in this book should be approached with an open mind, studied carefully and critically considered taking full responsibility for your health and well-being.

An important book that will help children to learn how changing their thinking can heal their lives.

-Dr David R Hamilton
Your Mind Can Heal Your Body, Why Kindness is Good For You.
Published by Hay House
www.drdavidhamilton.co.uk

Charan has found a charming way to teach children how we are all connected and empower them to make a positive difference for themselves and the world. With fun drawings, familiar situations and engaging questions along the way, the book becomes a personal experience for each child, ensuring that the effects are even more profound. Well done!

-Brad Yates
The Wizard's Wish: Or, How He Made the Yuckies Go Away
www.thewizardswish.com

At last, a children's book that makes energy work accessible and understandable. At last a children's book that will raise the vibration of their emotions and teach them to take responsibility for how they feel. Charan has done a beautiful job of connecting, how to transform your emotions and they way that you feel, in a language that children will understand and relate to. She has an excellent understanding of children and of this kind of work, bringing it together beautifully in this book. I often say that change needs to start with the children, and this book will empower children to take responsibility for themselves, and to be happier and more positive. I highly recommend it.

-Sasha Allenby
Co-author, Matrix Reimprinting Using EFT
Published by Hay House
www.matrixreimprintingbook.com

Charan has an open heart filled with love, combined with her natural born healing abilities, she has written a magical, purposeful book for children. Charan guides children toward love and teaches them how to turn a problem into a beautiful lesson with the concept of Ho'oponopono, an ancient Hawaiian method of healing. This is the first book I've read that takes a powerful healing method and makes it easy-to-understand by telling a mesmerizing story. Charan is a genius storyteller, intuitive and incredible teacher. I love this book because it teaches on so many different levels. I highly recommend Heba the Ho'oponoponist for children and anyone who loves children.

-Susan Barnes
Author of 8 books, International speaker and Workshop Leader.
www.susanbarnesauthor.com/

With lightness of heart, delight and an ever present love, this book brings the wisdom of a knowing soul to entreat the young heart of a child. I look forward to a signed copy to share with my young students. Their smiles will be guaranteed!!

Rose Marie Raccioppi MS FABI
Founder/Director of APOGEE Learning Enhancement Training Systems™
www.apogeelearning.com/
www.apogeelearning.blogspot.com/

There can be no greater lesson for a child than knowing that we are all connected and that we are powerful in our lovingness. This awareness changes lives. Charan's book makes this message so clear and so easy for children and adults of all ages to understand. It's beautifully written and the message unfolds delightfully! I can't wait to read it again and again!"

Victoria Michaels, CFSP
President/Founder Savvy Solutions, Inc.
www.savvysolutionsinc.net

Recommendations:

Till Schilling and Tappy Bear, a true tapping companion

www.tappybear.com

Paul Widdershoven:
Great Resources for kids;

www.imagr8kid.com

www.schoolmademucheasier.com

Ho'oponopono Cleaning Services;
www.icebluecleaning.com

Tapping Away the Blues – You Have The Power at Your Fingertips!
- Jayne Ferreira
www.tappingawaytheblues.com

It's Your Choice: Uncover Your Brilliance Using The Iceberg Process
 - Annie Cap
www.anniecap.co.uk

To my son, Hakam,

and to all the 'big' and 'small' children of the world.

Acknowledgments

First I want to thank my mum and dad, who started me on a spiritual journey very young. Heba, wouldn't be here without them.

Thanks to Dr Len for sharing his story to the world and teaching Ho'oponopono, and to Dr Joe Vitale for sharing it in his book Zero Limits.

I have to thank my wonderful friends and peers, from my Mastermind group, for all the support, and keeping me focused with this book. They were there for me every step of the way.

Paul Zelizer www.paulzelizer.com
Elmdea Bean www.elmdeabean.com
Charlotte Kamman http://charlottekamman.com/
Lindsay Murdoch www.lindsaymurdoch.com
Ilana Wolfson www.budgethepudge.com

Thanks to David Hamilton, and Susan Barnes for all the support from the beginning.

My special friends, who helped in more ways then they would know, with support and encouragement:
Deborah Hughes, Karen Richards, Kat Waring www.artofallowing.co.uk, Giia Weigel, Annie Cap and Guy Power, a marketing genius.

To Geoff Lam, Lucie Nguyen, owners of Saint Caffe www.SaintCaffe.com, where I enjoyed the best hot chocolate in the world while writing this book! Also to Jared Sayles who was always so attentive to my needs in the cafe.

All friends and family everywhere!

Have you had days where you feel upset because of something that has happened to you, like being called names , or bullied, or teased or even feeling ill? Or maybe something that you see happening to others, who are ill, poor, or are not being treated nicely? It could be anything, as it is hard when you experience any of these things. But how would you like to know that there is a way to feel good again, whether things on the outside change or not. It is about feeling good and peaceful inside. Kind of like that feeling when you go to the beach and play in the sea and sand, and you feel your feet in the sea or the joy of making a sandcastle. Can you feel that feeling in your body? Where do you feel it? Isn't it wonderful? We can call this feeling "bubbles", so that any time you read the word "bubbles", you will remember this wonderful feeling. You can experience this feeling all the time, no matter what is going on around you. But the secret is....... oh, I think I will wait till the end to tell you the BIG secret!

First I am going to tell you a story about Annie. She had a sister called Lucy. Lucy was younger than Annie. They shared their toys and other things, but sometimes they would argue: when Annie had one thing, Lucy wanted it as well.

Do you do that as well, if you have a brother or sister or a cousin? Well, Annie and Lucy sure did.

Annie went to school, and enjoyed school a lot; but there were some children that were not very nice to her. Some days they would call her names. She didn't like that.

Does that happen to you too, when you go to school or anywhere else? Are there some children or adults who are not very nice to you? It sure did happen to Annie.

One day Annie was teased by a girl in school, called Tisha, who called her some not very nice names, and took Annie's favourite pencil from her pencil case. Of course, this made Annie very sad, as she didn't like what Tisha had done. The names she had been called did not make her happy, and she had her favourite pencil taken from her as well. Her heart was feeling sad, hurt and angry too. She could feel it moving into her body. Kind of the same feeling like when you fall and hurt yourself, except this time it hurts in the heart. She definitely didn't have that happy "bubbles" feeling.

Does this happen to you when someone in school or at home is not very nice to you? It sure did happen to Annie.

Well, that day Annie went home from school, had her tea, and played with Lucy. But this was no normal evening. Something special was going to happen that night. Annie had no idea about this. Don't tell her, but we will soon find out what it was . . .

Well, that night Annie and Lucy went to bed. Mum came to read them a story, and then tucked them into their comfy beds.

It was no normal night because Annie was going to have a special visitor . . . do you want to know who it was? Well, listen carefully, as I am about to tell you.

Annie went to sleep quickly, as she was exhausted because of the things that had happened that day. As she fell into a deep sleep, she felt this tug on her ear. Pull, pull, pull, who was this pulling at her ear?

Annie opened her eyes slowly and there on her pillow was a little fairy, making fluttering noises with her wings. This fairy was beautifully different: she had gorgeous flowers in her hair, a chain of colourful flowers around her neck and a green grass skirt.

"Who are you?" Annie asked, rubbing her eyes.

"My name is Heba. I come from Hawaii!" she said.

"Do you mean that you travelled all this way for me?" asked Annie, as Hawaii was a long way from Annie's house.

Heba laughed, a cute little laugh, as she flew up in the air above Annie's head and sat between Annie's eyes, making her go cross-eyed as she tried to focus on Heba.

"I can go anywhere I want. I just have to think about it and I am there. I don't need to travel like you do. I go where I am needed, and where the message I have needs to be shared," she replied, still giggling.

Annie was curious. She sat up, while Heba floated near her, with her little wings fluttering in front of Annie's face.

"What message do you have for me and why do I need you?" Annie asked, confused.

Heba said, "Well, when you felt sad today, because of what happened to you, I received a message to come to you, and now I am here to show you something very magical. It is called Ho'oponopono!"

"What? Ho'o what?" laughed Annie.

"Say Ho, then opono, and then pono!" giggled Heba.

Annie followed. "Ho...opono...pono, well, that wasn't hard."

You try it: say Ho, then opono, and then pono. Ho'oponopono. See, it's not hard, is it? Well done for trying it!

Annie was now even more curious, and wondered how Heba knew she was upset. So she asked Heba, "How did you know I was upset?".

"Because once you know the magic secret, you will see how we are all connected by magic threads, kind of like strings that are made of light, except we can't see them. If you open yourself up by listening with your heart, you can know too. But hang on, I need to take you to a magical place, where you will see for yourself what I mean. Are you ready to come with me, Annie?" Heba asked.

Annie said in wonderment, "Yes I am, Heba, but how?"

"Don't worry. This is all happening in your dream, and you can do anything you like in your dreams; fly too! Also, I have this magic flying rainbow dust" replied Heba, as she waved her wand and Annie was covered in rainbow coloured dust!

Annie began to notice herself floating above her bed, and it felt like fun! Wow! So off they went through the window and out into the starry night, with the smiling moon up high in the sky.

Annie felt free, and light. Together Heba and Annie flew higher and higher, until everything below them was as small as toy houses and cars. As they flew, Annie was surprised how the flying seemed to be happening all on its own. Ahead of them in the night sky, Annie saw a glowing light. They were gently flying towards this light, which was getting brighter and brighter as they got closer.

Then suddenly, as if by magic, the light had come towards them at such incredible speed. They were wrapped into this light, which felt warm and loving, like a fluffy, cosy blanket. Annie felt as if her heart was filled with a golden light spreading through her body; she had never felt this feeling as deeply as she did right now. It was like the "bubbles" feeling, but a million times bigger!

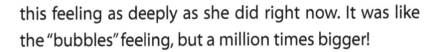

Just as fast as they had entered the light, they were out on the other side of it, and Annie was still feeling the huge "bubbles" feeling in and around her.

On this side of the light you could see things that you couldn't on the other side.

Annie asked Heba, "What is that big ball of light that we just came through?" as they floated on air in what seemed to be the night sky. Heba replied, "We all came from that ball of light: it is the Source of all things on Earth, and in the Universe. Some call it God, some call it the Universal Energy."

Do you know what Source is? If you think of a big candle flame, that flame can light many other candles. In the same way this big ball of light is the big flame, and all the little flames come from this big flame. Everything begins and ends with this big ball of light.

They watched hundreds of little lights coming out of the ball, while other lights were going in and merging with it. Lights going out and lights going in, kind of like a road where cars go one way and the other. Heba explained that the ones coming off were souls to be born, and the ones going in were souls that just left their bodies. But she explained that this light was in trees, grass, water, and everything else we see around us. If it wasn't for Source, there would be nothing. So everything we see is really us. When we are born, and we grow up, we see people and things around us as separate, but really that is an illusion, kind of like a magician's trick where you think something is real but it isn't. Yes, we look different, as lights can be of different shapes, sizes, and colours too, but light is light!

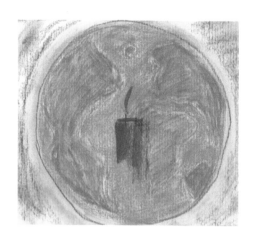

Annie was staring in amazement at this beautiful light. She understood now that we are all One, like little candles coming off a big fire, and that on Earth we look around, and just because we see others with different faces, or skin colour, we assume we are different. But really we are One!

Heba was smiling, as she was pleased that Annie was able to understand now. She added, "When we feel that others treat us in a way that is not nice, which hurts our feelings, we can remember that we are all from the same big light, even though others don't realise this. But if we remember we are the same light, then that helps others remember too, because you begin to shine the light of the Source, and that reminds others of their light in a magical way."

"How do we do that?" asked Annie.

"Well, now that you can see we are all connected, and One, let me show you, looking from here down onto Earth, what that looks like," Heba replied.

Heba flew off, and called out to Annie to fly behind her, but, as before, Annie just followed without having to do anything. It was SO much fun, just floating and going places. The thing that surprised Annie was how that feeling of love, peace and "bubbles" was still with her, even after moving away from the Source.

As they flew in this Space, they approached Earth, a beautiful blue planet, and Annie saw how these lights that had come from Source were going towards Earth, and lights leaving Earth were going back to Source. As they got closer, she saw something else she had never seen before – she saw the connections between everything.

Hovering above the globe, Heba said, "Look at the way we are all connected: to Earth, to other people, to animals, whether we are on opposite sides of the planet or close to one another." Annie saw how dolphins knew where to go in the ocean, and how geese knew how to make that beautiful shape in the sky, and how bees knew which flower to go to and then get back to their beehive, as everything is connected, and animals, insects and little critters use this inner knowing or intelligence to get around.

Can you think of other examples of this to share?

Heba said, "This is built-in intelligence, that we all have. If we feel it in our hearts, we can feel the connections, that allow us to use our built-in intelligence too, just like the animals and this is what is called the genius mind."

As she said this, Annie began to notice connections between all things, as strings of light linked to everything. Heba laughed, as she saw Annie's face drop in surprise at the idea of all things and people being connected to one another.

Heba asked Annie to look above Earth: she saw a massive transparent object. This, in turn, was also connected to Source. Big letters on it read, "MEMORY BANK". In there were memories of all problems, troubles and illnesses, everything you could think of. These memories were all shut in there, but had tubes of light connected to each and every human on the planet.

Annie saw how this tube of light was connected to her; memories of Tisha, everyone she had ever met, or not met, but even things that we think are not alive, like cars, trains, planes, chairs, tables, and our clothes too! All connected to her. She asked Heba how this could be, that all the memories of other people, animals and things were connected to her?

Heba replied, "You see, we are all One. You know that now, as you have seen it. We share this MEMORY BANK and if we take responsibility for whatever is in it, we can clear this MEMORY BANK! ".

Annie was quiet, as she was trying to understand what Heba was telling her.

Heba then took her back to the time where she had been teased. Annie was looking down at herself in that situation, and she saw how hurt she was by it all. But, this time, she saw the light connection between Tisha and her, and others too! Everyone had the same light. Heba said, "Can you see that you and Tisha are the same light on the inside, but both of you just have different bodies?"

Annie just nodded quietly, as she was still amazed.

Are you able to get a feel of what Annie is noticing? Maybe you can see that you are connected to everyone in your life, and know now that we are all One. The problems we experience, or others around us experience, are all connected in the MEMORY BANK. So we can clear the shared memories in the MEMORY BANK as every single memory is stored there, even the hurt that a little bird would feel if it couldn't find food or even the children in Africa that go hungry every day.

Wow, this was a big one for Annie to absorb, but she was getting it. Are you?

Annie asked Heba, "So what can I do to help?"

Heba replied, "It's easy. You say thank you and I love you. Then you will see a wonderful thing happening. The memories in the MEMORY BANK will begin to clear!"

"So who am I saying that to?" asked Annie.

"You are speaking to the Source, you come from it and it lives in you," Heba replied.

Annie repeated in her mind: "Thank you and I love you, thank you and I love you". As she spoke, she saw a light coming from Source go into this MEMORY BANK, clearing the memories to do with Tisha, and she saw how that was connected to memories of the past and future, all being zapped with this light like a magic wand would do, leaving in their place a glowing light of peace and calm.

Heba said, "You see, you just gave Source permission to clear the memories, by just saying the phrases!"

"We all have ups and downs in our lives, as we go through school, or later on when we grow up, but we can remove the memories in the MEMORY BANK by allowing Source to vacuum them out!" Heba said.

"But you must remember," Heba added, "that as you do this, you must have no expectations as to what will happen. All you need to know is that you are helping so many as well as yourself, in ways that would surprise you, just by clearing the MEMORY BANK. So remember, repeat the phrases, and watch for those surprises that will come to you in Divine timing." Heba cheekily winked at Annie as she said this.

"What is Divine timing?" Annie asked.

"It is when everything happens perfectly, people and events come together in a way we would have never have thought of. This happens with perfect timing, and when it is right for us. My visit to you, Annie, was in Divine timing too, as it was the right time to show you all this. This is what Divine timing is," replied Heba.

As she repeated those phrases, Annie felt as if a light had switched on in Tisha, like turning on a light bulb, and she began to smile. Heba showed Annie how, now that Tisha remembered who she really was, she began to be nice to Annie and others.

By repeating "Thank you and I love you", you remove memories from the MEMORY BANK, and, as you do this, whatever the outcome, it will be good because you begin to shine your light, allowing others to shine their light, which can only bring happy smiles to their faces. Just like you shine a torch in the dark, it makes you happy to be able to see around you? Well, you kind of become a torch and let others switch on their own torches inside! Isn't that great? When people are not happy, it is because they are in the dark. So, by seeing their own torch light shine, they see through their darkness!

Heba said, " You can say this to the chair you sit on, the house you live in, the car or plane or train you travel on, they are all from Source, just like the trees, the flowers, animals, the ocean, your clothes and everything you can see or feel. They all have memories in the MEMORY BANK too, so by saying "Thank you and I love you", you are helping the planet as a whole, by clearing the memories in there. You might not see how, but you know now that it does. Not only that, but by saying thank you, you are being grateful for everything in your life, and, as the memories get cleared, you attract experiences aligned with your Divine nature. You may have some days where you feel that it isn't doing anything, but keep saying these phrases, "Thank you and I love you", and you will feel peaceful. When you feel peaceful, then you are happy, no matter what is going on around you."

Annie gave Heba a big hug and said, "Thank you for sharing this with me!" Heba smiled and hugged her back, saying, "You are so welcome, Annie. Now you know what Ho'oponopono is all about. This is your gift today, as my name means Gift from God in Hawaiian."

Now you know the secret, will you use it, just like Annie is going to? You too know how Ho'oponopono works now.

Next thing Annie knew was that she was being woken up by her mum with a big hug in the morning, to go to school.

Annie woke up wondering about her dream, whether it was real! She looked on her pillow and there was a flower that she remembered seeing in Heba's hair. Also she found magic rainbow dust sprinkled in her hair! She was sure then that it must have really happened.

That day at school she was amazed to see the same scene she had seen the night before, where Tisha seemed happier and didn't bother her!

Heba wants you to know, that this message is for you also, as she might come and visit you one night as a surprise, just to see how you are getting on with it!

So that is the story of Annie and Heba the Ho'oponoponoist. Now you know what Ho'oponopono is, why don't you try this for yourself, but remember the three important rules:

1. We are all from the same Source, and have that shining light within us. You have it, just like Annie, or anyone else and you are perfect and amazing in every way.

2. We are responsible for all the memories in the MEMORY BANK and for all that we experience in our life. Even the memories connected to our clothes, cars, trains, chairs, tables, plants, computers, and the water you drink too, everything. Water is so important, as a big part of our body is made of it. So if, when we drink it (and we should drink plenty!), we say "Thank you and I love you" to it, it will go into our body, into every part of our body, helping us to stay healthy and letting our light shine brightly.

3. We repeat "Thank you and I love you", and that clears the memories in the MEMORY BANK, so that we are able to shine our inner lights like switching on a torch, and it reminds others to switch on their torch too. Remember, it only takes one person to change the world: why not you?

This is Heba's gift to you too.

"I thank you and I love you!"

This is a beautiful visualisation that I have created for you, that takes you on a journey with a dolphin to help you release any emotions you might want to let go of, and to receive the gift of Ho'oponopono.
Go to www.hebathehoop.com/gift.htm (case sensitive)

You might also like www.hebathehoop.com

Enjoy!

Charan

I Love You

www.charansurdhar.com

9 780956 485106